HOLLYWOOD MISOGYNY

♂Niccolò

Hollywood Misogyny
by ♂Niccolò di Bernardo dei Machiavelli

© 2019 by Juleon Schins. All rights reserved.
No part of this publication may be reproduced, stored in a retrieval system or transmitted in any way by any means, electronic, mechanical, photocopy, recording or otherwise without the prior permission of the author except as provided by US copyright law.

ISBN 978-1-64550-007-0 (Paperback)

CONTENTS

Introduction: Zeta-Jones, Jolie, and Bullock   i

Chapter 1:   Hollywood and Meg Ryan   1

Chapter 2:   Hollywood and Gal Gadot   7

Chapter 3:   Hollywood and Feminism   17

Chapter 4:   Hollywood and Religion   29

Appendix: Rotten-Tomatoes Appreciation
                of Cahiers-elected Movies   37

Epilogue: Why Women Do Not Unite   87

This book is part of a 2019 decalogue consisting of

- Sign of Times: Music Anthology and Lyric Analysis
- Hollywood Misogyny
- Beginners' Guide to the FED:
  Why it is Unique on our Planet
- The Kennedy Kurse: Four Obvious Konnektions
- Manichaeism and Satanic Child Abuse
- Progressive Intolerance: Last Stop Before Hitler
- Patriotic Ingenuousness
- Deism versus Theism:
  2-7 in the Scientific Arena of the 20th Century
- Feminine Feminist: A Missing Link Eluding Discovery
- The Snake: Three Millennia of Anti-Semitism

Dedicated to ♀

INTRODUCTION

Zeta-Jones, Jolie, and Bullock

Second wave feminism, the slut of male misogyny, erased the term "femininity" from the dictionary many decades ago. In my dictionary though, "femininity" survived,[1] as a term referring to weaker-sex elegance[2] in public behavior, characterized by discretion, serviceability, a quasi-mystical power to sympathize with children, a human-affection centered creativity, and, both last and least, by a correct judgment of the anthropomorphic status of male sexual appetite.[3]

---

1   As it did in the MS-Word dictionary: the word shows no red wiggly underscores
2   Male elegance exists with the same right as female elegance. Both elegances are determined by human biology, though, and are therefore by definition completely different. Only nerds and animals judge otherwise.
3   This "correct judgment" places men's sexual needs where they belong, and that is far below the tenth priority. Girls that fail to do so, and place it too high, end up miserable, in the best of cases. Obviously, the judgment varies for girls, for unmarried women, and for mothers. Especially girls, from the age of 12 onwards, need parental guidance in learning how to establish non-exclusive friendships with several boys, while delaying sexual intercourse until at least the age of 20. Mind, this latter aspect is not meant

In this introduction, I try to come up with some reasons why Hollywood is and always has been a gender-brainwashing machine, since long before second wave feminism. Hollywood strategically forces female movie stars into either vulgar sexual, degradingly subjected, or would-be-male roles: in general, anything that leads to the disappearance of femininity. I will make my point for three exquisitely feminine girls who became famous actresses: Catherine Zeta-Jones, Sandra Bullock, and Angelina Jolie.

Let us start out with the Welsh lady, **Catherine Zeta-Jones**, widely considered to be the most beautiful woman on this planet (I join the choir). Catherine is involved in many works of charity: especially in her native country, Wales. I especially admire her efforts with respect to fighting abuse of children, a phenomenon whose horror and scale very few people realize. She says of herself that she is naturally shy, which is nothing but an exquisite expression of femininity. On the other hand, on-screen, Catherine is forced to wear a degrading décolleté. At her age it is no shame to actually *look like a woman of her age*. So what is the décolleté meant for? To compensate for age-lost beauty? Or is it, like nearly always, just another expression of Hollywood's misogyny? In her 2009 movie "Rebound", Catherine is forced to cripple her femininity continuously. Her role is a direct insult to womanhood. I do not inquire

---

discriminatorily: it holds for boys, too. Look at the statistics: less educated youngsters have sexual intercourse at younger ages, and make a mess of their marriages.

Zeta-Jones, Jolie, and Bullock

into the amount of pressure exerted on either Bart Freundlich or Catherine, to act her female role. Fact is that Catherine's femininity-crippling scenes are legion. To name but a few, there is the absurd scene in a boxing hall where two slaves of modernity are tearing each other apart, and Catherine stands up shouting something about kidneys.

Note that mister dirty-hands plays a clumsy clown, while the main aspect of Catherine's role is to take everything seriously. Who got her so deeply humiliated to wear that navel-deep décolleté?

The scene is not humoristic at all, and totally out of context: as if Hollywood wished to give the male public a good feeling of superiority over women. Second, the blind date begins literally on a "pee & shit" level. For example, Catherine's date gives her, for some unclear reason, a face massage, with the awkward suggestion that he did not wash his hands after having deposited. Third and worst, after the face massage he sticks his finger into her mouth, in a way that allows for but a single interpretation: that of a female sex slave performing *fellatio under shitty conditions*.[4]

Profoundly felt condolences. Hollywood has utterly destroyed Catherine, as a person and as a woman. Mark that she is rich enough to wave such roles away. So why is she making a fool out of herself after a splendid career? Finally, would Catherine feel no embarrassment to play the role of a "prude" 40+ lady, unable to believe in a relation with a 26-er, while her real-life husband has her daddy's age? She might be so professional that she has reached a total mental detachment from her role.

My own guess, however, is that she is simply *blackmailed* by misogynic Hollywood, which requires her to play the pathetic woman who abhors of losing beauty with age, and is rapidly losing her wits. What Hollywood promotes, is young ladies marrying rich, but toothless impotent cripples wearing dark glasses.[5] Hollywood does *not like* old rich ladies with a toy-boy. And as far as the above movie-still is concerned, a décolleté down to the navel is both ultra-sexual

---

[4] Does Catherine have the slightest idea of how many millions of female sex slaves are daily forced to do what her dirty movie makes tasteless fun of?

[5] Think of Karl Lagerfeld, better known as King Ridicule

Zeta-Jones, Jolie, and Bullock   v

and anti-feminine. Catherine Zeta-Jones fully confirms my Hollywood claim.

My second movie star is **Angelina Jolie**, shot below[6] at the "Global Summit to End Sexual Violence in Conflict". On screen, Angelina is unrecognizable. Nothing shows but explicit eroticism[7] and a totally denuded femininity.

Angelina represents the strongest confirmation of my Hollywood claim. Of course, she knows exactly what feelings she arouses, worldwide, with her erotic movies. Now who can tell me what dozens of erotic movies might ever contribute to "ending sexual violence in conflict"? Would she be telling the world that, without conflict, one should promote sexual violence? Else, her "classy" whore-like nude scenes plainly contradict her presence at that global summit.[8] Her stance is so utterly illogical that I personally believe she is blackmailed like all other effeminate women in Hollywood. In her case, the result is so demonic that I would

---

6   https://en.wikipedia.org/wiki/Angelina_Jolie
7   like Gia (1998), Playing by Heart (1998), Pushing Tin (1999), Original Sin (2001), Tomb Raider (2001), Life or Something Like It (2002), Taking Lives (2004), Alexander (2004), Mr. & Mrs. Smith (2005), and Beowulf (2007): they spare nipple nor pubic hair for the audience
8   There exists no trace of correlation between sexual violence and zones of conflict. It is only journalists that are sent to conflict zones for the purpose of recording violence (which is never gender-specific), which makes people think that in zones of conflict one genders suffers more than the other.

not be surprised that she was compelled to taking part in Hollywood secret devil-worshiping cults. It starts out "interesting", to be member of a secret club with many movie VIP's, it subsequently degrades women to blind nude-walking bodies with hoodies, and it ends up with executing orders.

Poor Angelina looks like a Madame Tussaud wax model. She underwent so many surgical operations that her beauty specialists could even have had a chimp look like that.

Angelina, in spite of all appearances I do believe in you. I think you are the very opposite of what you act like. Fight back against your ugly blackmailer, and loosen yourself from the grips of Hollywood.

Zeta-Jones, Jolie, and Bullock

Sandra Bullock seems the least Hollywood-destroyed of the triplet, as one cannot look into psyches. Anyway, *on screen* no lack of anti-femininity, and, although a little less than the previous two ladies, quite oversexed at times.

Fumbling went fine, mission accomplished

"Miss Congeniality" is one of her better movies.[9] A Special Agent for the FBI, she despises everything woman-like, with

---

9   Miss Congeniality is a 2000 American action comedy film directed by Donald Petrie, written by Marc Lawrence, Katie Ford, and Caryn Lucas, and starring Sandra Bullock with Michael Caine, Benjamin Bratt, William Shatner, Ernie Hudson, and Candice Bergen. Miss Congeniality was released by Warner Bros. Pictures on December 22, 2000 and was a box office hit grossing $212 million worldwide. Bullock also garnered a nomination for the Golden Globe Award for Best Actress – Motion Picture Comedy or Musical.

"the Hollywood-must" special disdain for housewives. In the movie Sandra receives a self-begged-for assignment from her FBI boss: to go undercover and participate as Miss New Jersey in a beauty pageant for Miss US in San Antonio, Texas. As Sandra's heart-felt aspiration is to be like a man (so dictated by sound second-wave feminism), she needs special education in female behavior.

This is kindly proportioned to her by (of course) a man.[10] He is charming, sarcastic, and continuously makes classical-style male jokes about females.

A clear example of "de-femininization" is that women should, like men, not blink when touched upon their breasts. As should be well known, the natural behavior of men is to encourage the female nurse to explore unknown fields. On the other hand, the natural female behavior is to firmly decline any male offer to touch her at all, and least of all, on those bodily parts that they have not in common with males.

Hence, the dictate of second-wave feminism is clear: although everything shouts out in your female body "keep your filthy claws off of me!", you do not blink, and act like a man. In my view this is as anti-natural as idiotic.

Since in reality (and in the movie) Sandra has too small a bra-size for impersonating a Miss beautiful, her "educator" proposes to insert two jelly cups between breast and bra. So proposed, so done. While dirty Harry is busy fumbling, Sandra doesn't blink.

---

10 Original? The "dark" Middle Ages were really fond of it. And of sexually tinted allusions. We simply did not change at all.

Just like an ordinary guy.[11] Too bad, Sandra, your masterpiece of feminism does not help a single mentally healthy woman on this planet.

In complete agreement with the mantra's of second wave feminism, Sandra responds to every step in her female education with rude sexism. Uncle Hollywood requires it exactly like that: there is still too large a fraction of the movie-crunching populace that refuses total brainwashing. Uncle Hollywood knows that endless repetition is the only basis of education (read: brainwashing).

As the competition begins, beauty-contestant Sandra impresses the judges with her male-crippling self-defense qualities. As the competition evolves, in her professional role of special Agent, Sandra comes to believe the pageant competition director is a copycat of a bomb-placer. In the final round, Sandra is stunned when she is named first runner up. Miss Rhode Island, Sandra's closest friend, wins the pageant and is nominated Miss United States. As she is being crowned with the rigged tiara by the competition director, Heidi-clothed Sandra suspects foul play, and interrupts the crowning ceremony with an abundant display of muscles. Thanks to yodel-dee-yodel-doo Sandra, the tiara explodes elsewhere, provoking wounds nor deaths.

The only aspect I really liked of this movie was that it makes second wave feminism look thoroughly ridiculous and inconsistent.

---

11 I believe this is the only moment in the movie she shows her true disgust: *by acting as if dirty Harry did not even exist.*

The above three examples of Hollywood-destroyed women introduce the reader into this book's main message: **Hollywood systematically cripples women's dignities, and exclusively allows movie fun at the cost of housewives, the uneducated, the poor, the prude romantics, and of all religions but Judaism.**

From the Hollywood veto on jokes concerning Judaism, it is quite easy to identify the religion of the owner. As is well known, Judaic culture had serious problems with misogyny in the times of Jesus. In case of adultery, the man was without sin, and the woman was to be stoned (at least according to the Judaic law). Hence she was taken to Jesus, and not the man, who was as much an adulterer as she.

Many Semitic peoples (Arabic, Phoenician, Hebrew, Aramaic, Maltese, and Philistine, to name only the northern linguistic part) not only had such misogyny in common, but also kept the tradition alive until today. This largely explains Hollywood's misogyny. These peoples traditionally consider women as male property. Nothing to be ashamed about: this behavior was universal. It only changed with Christ, as is obvious from the historical facts.

As a rule, for better legibility, **all quoted passages** are slightly indented and written in a different font as compared to the standard.

Chapter 1

Hollywood and Meg Ryan

Hollywood punishes the exquisitely feminine capacities for romance, for unlimited love for husband and children, and for creative intelligence.[12]

---

12 Female intelligence is not weaker than male intelligence, whatever chessboard and cooking championships might suggest. Female intelligent creativity concentrates on animated beings, the male on bricks and other soulless beings

The information of this Chapter is mostly taken from the Wikipedia website on Meg Ryan.[13]

Born Margaret Mary Emily Hyra (November 19, 1961), Meg Ryan was raised in Fairfield, Connecticut, the daughter of Susan Jordan (née Duggan), a former actress and English teacher, and Harry Hyra, a math teacher. She is of mixed European (German, Irish, and Polish) descent. She was raised Catholic and attended St. Pius X Elementary School in Fairfield. She has two sisters, Dana and Annie, and a brother, musician Andrew Hyra, a member of the band *Billy Pilgrim*. Her parents divorced in 1976 when she was 15 years old. The unavoidable years preceding the divorce must have been an enormous nightmare for her, if not a straight youth trauma. One may estimate that trauma by the duration of her own marriage (two years).

Ryan graduated from Bethel High School in 1979. She studied journalism as an undergraduate, first at the University of Connecticut and then at New York University. During college, she acted in television commercials and the soap opera As the World Turns to earn extra money. Due to her success as an actress, she dropped out of college a semester before she planned to graduate. When she joined the Screen Actors Guild, she used the surname "Ryan", her grandmother's maiden name. From a short-lived marriage to junkie Dennis Quaid (1991-2001), she gave birth to Jack Quaid, who uses his father's surname. In January 2006, Ryan adopted a 14-month-old girl from China whom she named Daisy True.

---

13 https://en.wikipedia.org/wiki/Meg_Ryan

Hollywood and Meg Ryan

Ryan quickly established herself, both nationally and internationally, as a most successful actresses in the 1990s, particularly in romantic comedy films. All her romantic movies are automatically dubbed "come-dies", although to my taste not even half of them qualify as a comedy. For a movie to be a comedy it is simply not enough to contain some jokes and funny, unexpected situations.

However, this is what Hollywood dictates. Its misogyny is comparable to that in the ancient Jewish culture at the time of Moses, when women were considered as mere property. Like any other piece of furniture, they had no right testify in court as witnesses.

Ryan's commercial successes all occurred in the decade 1998–1999. Her first successful leading role was the 1989 romantic comedy film "When Harry Met Sally", which paired her with comedic leading man Billy Crystal and earned her a Golden Globe nomination. Her portrayal of Sally Albright includes an oft-recounted scene in which Sally, lunching with Harry in Katz's Delicatessen in Manhattan, theatrically demonstrates how easy it is for a woman to fake an orgasm. The 1993 enormously successful romance "Sleepless in Seattle" paired Ryan for a second time with Tom Hanks (the first time being in the commercial disappointment, which later developed a cult following, "Joe Vs the Volcano". She made an excellent choice by rejecting the offer to play Clarice Starling in 1991, for The Silence of the Lambs. Although the latter is a spectacular movie, Meg did not have the talent to play in gruesome movies. In 1994, Ryan took a role that differed from the romantic-comedy ingénue character for which she had become famous. Luis Mandoki's When a Man Loves a Woman, a romantic social drama film also starring Andy Garcia, she played an alcoholic high-school guidance counselor. The film and her performance were both well received by critics. One critic called the film "a first-class production, accentuated by fine performances and an unflinching script", and another praised Ryan for her "roller-coaster role". The film was grossed $50 million in the United States alone, and garnered the actress her first Screen Actors Guild Award. The same year 1994, Ryan returned to type, starring alongside Tim Robbins in Fred Schepisi's romantic comedy. The film centers on a mechanic and a Princeton doctoral candidate who fall in love, with the aid of the graduate student's uncle, Albert Einstein (played by Walter Matthau). In 1995, critic Richard Corliss called her "the current soul of romantic comedy". That same year, she appeared opposite Kevin Kline in Lawrence Kasdan's French Kiss, a romance that catered to her "America's Sweetheart" image. Ryan received the Women in Film Crystal Award. In 1996, Ryan starred in the film Courage under Fire alongside Denzel Washington and Matt Damon. The following year, she voiced the lead role in the animated film Anastasia, which garnered good reviews and enjoyed box office success. She also appeared opposite Matthew Broderick in "Addicted to Love", playing a female lead at least superficially different from her usual direction, as one of a pair of jilted lovers bent on revenge. In 1998, she starred in two films. "City of Angels" drew positive reviews and became a financial success, topping nearly $200 million worldwide.

"You've Got Mail" for the third time paired Ryan with Hanks, earning her a third Golden Globe nomination and making over $250 million worldwide. She also appeared in 1998's Hurlyburly with Sean Penn. In 2001 she starred in her last romantic success comedy with Kate & Leopold, alongside Hugh Jackman. A film about a British Duke who t ravels through time from New York in 1876 to the present and falls in love with a successful market researcher in the modern New York, the James Mangold-directed film received a positive response, with Lael Loewenstein of Variety summing it as "a mostly charming and diverting tale." At a total gross of $70 million, it would be Ryan's highest-grossing film of the decade.

Since 2003, Ryan would break away from her usual roles. That marked the end of her career. To me, this is a clear sign of Hollywood blackmail. Misogynic Hollywood does not like successful and attractive women play roles in which female empathic excellence is displayed.

In the case of Céline Dion this is even more overtly the case: her way of clothing, in all her concerts, was always exquisitely feminine: once she even dressed what was popular in the nineteenth century. Then, suddenly seeing her promoting a gender-effacing business, is sufficient proof to me of plain Hollywood misogynic blackmail. Useless, evidently, to ask these ladies whether they were blackmailed: that is inherent to being blackmailed. Would one confirm, then all the threats would be mercilessly applied. Of course, not immediately, but a year later, and in such a way, that all murders have appear like mere accidents. The typical punishment is to leave the blackmailed person alive, while killing all her loved ones.

By the way, is anything left of her genderless babywear line? All photos have been taken off the web: a quite usual phenomenon with blackmailing.

Céline Dion, before

and after being blackmailed

From a highly concentrated, very professional singer, to a sadly looking, too old lady for her "décolleté".

CHAPTER 2

Hollywood and Gal Gadot

2.1 Six Classic Banned Movies

Below I a reproduce a March 2018 review written on the web about **Hollywood-banned** movies, by Christopher McKittrick.[14]

> These days, with the right streaming service, it's possible to watch virtually any movie ever made. However, that obviously wasn't always the case, particularly when films were banned in a particular country or region. In the days before home video and digital distribution, banning a film in a particular area meant that audiences really couldn't see it — unless they traveled far enough outside of the ban. While banning films is less common today, some countries (especially those without open access to the internet) continue to limit access to movies that authorities want to keep out of the public eye. Generally, films have been banned by authorities for political or religious reasons, with the dominant political party or religious institution deeming the content of a film "offensive" or subversive and subsequently preventing the public from viewing the film.

---

[14] https://www.thoughtco.com/classic-banned-movies-4158693

In other cases, a film might be banned because its content is deemed obscene (nudity, violence, gore, etc.) This is not only done to "protect" audiences from gruesome material, but also to prevent potential copycat actions based on the material in the film. Ultimately, studios want to avoid bans because it cuts into the worldwide box office earnings. In most cases today studios are willing to find a compromise instead of accepting a ban. For example, several U.S. films (such as "Django Unchained") agreed to extensive edits to get approval for release in China, while others are banned regardless. These are six films that have been banned from cinemas for various reasons.

All Quiet on the Western Front (1930)

The film All Quiet on the Western Front, which was adapted from the famous Erich Maria Remarque novel, was considered a monumental success upon release and later won two Academy Awards. The epic depicts the horrors of World War I, and was released only a dozen years removed from that conflict (and only nine years before an even deadlier World War would engulf the globe). Not every country appreciated this on-screen representation of World War I. The German Nazi Party believed that the film was anti-German and, after several screenings that were disrupted by Nazi brown shirts, *All Quiet on the Western Front* was banned. Similarly, it was banned in Italy and Austria for being anti-Fascist and in New Zealand and Australia for graphic content and being anti-war. The movie was also banned parts of France. Curiously, the film was also banned in Poland — allegedly for being viewed as too pro-German. All bans on the film have since been lifted, but in the immediate aftermath Hollywood was very concerned about releasing other films that would be banned in lucrative markets like Germany. Hollywood would not produce a clearly anti-Nazi feature until Warner Bros. released 1939's *Confessions of a Nazi Spy* (unsurprisingly, that film was banned by Germany and its allies).

Duck Soup (1933)

The hilarious Marx Brothers frequently found their anarchic brand of comedy under fire for its ridiculousness — for example, their 1931 film *Monkey Business* was banned in Ireland out of concerns that it might encourage anarchy. Later in the 1930s, the Marx Brothers' movies also received a general ban in Germany because the brothers were Jewish. The most significant ban that the brothers faced was for their 1933 comedic masterpiece *Duck Soup*. In the film, Groucho Marx is appointed leader of a small country named Freedonia and his wild regime soon puts him at odds with neighboring Sylvania. Italian dictator Benito Mussolini believed *Duck Soup* was an attack on his regime and banned the film in Italy, a fact that the Marx brothers were reportedly delighted about — because in fact they *had* intended the film as a send-up of fascist regimes like Mussolini's!

Some Like It Hot (1959)

Much of the plot involves Curtis and Lemmon dressing as women to escape after bearing witness to a mob killing. However, the cross-dressing did not go over well in Kansas — during the initial release *Some Like It Hot* was banned in Kansas for being "disturbing."

A Clockwork Orange (1971)

Stanley Kubrick's *A Clockwork Orange*, which is based on the 1962 novel by Anthony Burgess, focuses on a juvenile delinquent who, after a spree of sexual and physical violence, is "cured" by undergoing intense psychological treatment. The nudity and violence in the film led to general bans in several countries, including Ireland, Singapore, South Africa, and South Korea.

Monty Python's Life of Brian (1979)

A satire on religion by famed comedy troupe Monty Python was always bound to be controversial, but *Life of Brian* —about a man born in the manger next to Jesus and who is mistaken for the Messiah— was met with ire by religious authorities in many countries. *Life of Brian* was banned in Ireland, Malaysia, Norway, Singapore, South Africa, and some cities in the United Kingdom.

Wonder Woman (2017)

2017's *Wonder Woman* was banned in Lebanon, Qatar, and Tunisia in spite of its enormous popularity elsewhere. The primary reason for the ban in these countries was political. *Wonder Woman* star Gal Gadot is Israeli, and prior to her movie career she served in the Israel Defense Forces. Because of the significant political differences between these three countries and Israel, authorities did not want to promote a movie featuring someone who is so closely identified with Israel.

2.2 Hollywood and Israel

Until here McKittrick's article. To me it sounds cinematographically unbiased. If that is indeed the case (everybody is obviously allowed to be biased), the following questions occur to me.

First, Hollywood has no problem with a non-Jewish religious satire, yet it bans a PG-13 movie because the lead role is played by an Israeli ex-military. In general, Hollywood allows all religions to be satirized, except Judaism. Likewise, Hollywood allows all nations to be satirized, even the US, except Israel.

Second, *All Quiet on the Western Front*, which was adapted from the famous Erich Maria Remarque novel about Word War I, was a monumental success upon release and later won two Academy Awards; yet, it was banned by Hollywood, for a reason I ignore, while it was also banned in most European countries for the most contradictory of reasons. According to McKittrick: "The German Nazi Party believed that the film was anti-German and, after several screenings that were disrupted by Nazi brown shirts, *All Quiet on the Western Front* was banned. Similarly, it was banned in Italy and Austria for being anti-Fascist and in New Zealand and Australia for graphic content and being anti-war. The movie was also banned [in] parts of France. Curiously, the film was also banned in Poland — allegedly for being viewed as too pro-German."

If I understand McKittrick correctly, Germany and Austria ban it for being anti-brown, Italy for being anti-Fascist (sorry McKittrick, but in the interbellum the average Austrian had no clue of the meaning of "Fascism"), in France and Hollywood for unknown reasons, and in New Zealand and Australia for being anti-war (sic)![15]

If one thing is clear, then it is that all banners themselves were pretty sick in their minds, most probably due to an overdose of local political correctness.

Too bad, McKittrick does not mention the movie's ban in Israel. Is Israel not supposed to be a democratic country in favor of freedom of expression, at least, for the Jewish population? Or would Israeli's consider the movie too pro-German?

---

[15] Oops. In what short time society can change its mind.

Chapter 3

Hollywood and Feminism

US Feminism comes in so-called "waves":

(i) *First-wave feminism* is the social fight for gender-independent civil rights, mainly active and passive voting and property rights. These goals were largely achieved in the US by 1960, and did justice to women in general.

(ii) *Second-wave feminism* is the social fight for legalization of provoked abortion and woman-preferential adaptation of the divorce law (children in principle stay with their mother, unless proven unable to raise them), and lasted from the 1960's to the 1980's. These goals are morally abject. They have led to the enormous amount of single mothers, who suffer the worst humiliations to raise their children on their own. Moreover, they have totally demolished the last defense against being men's sex slaves: most abortions are clearly due to the man's pressure on the woman *not to conceive*. Conception means a lot to a mother, when backed by a loving husband. To 80% of men, conception means less sexual availability of their girlfriend, and the terrible annoyance of a little shitter annex shouter with human pretenses.

(iii) *Third-wave feminism* is not a social fight, but a bunch of mediocre social theories discussing neologisms like "intersectionality", "sex positivity", "vegetarian ecofeminism", "transfeminism", and "postmodern feminism". It is a thin veil hiding the abjectness of second wave feminism.

(iv) *Fourth-wave feminism* is a social fight aimed at eliminating psychological and, as far as possible, physical differences between the two sexes. Its ideal is to transform the digital concepts of gender and sex into continuous concepts. These, too, are abject goals.

In this book I propose to reduce the acceptation of "feminism" to merely two colors:

(i) *Altruistic Feminism* is a social fight for the well-being of *all women*.

(ii) *Feminism sec* is a social fight for the well-being of only those VIP women, who occupy high-profile positions in politics, journalism, and large companies; it is characterized by extreme egotism, and a rabid, irrational contempt of motherhood.

In my view, a feminist is comparable to a pedophile priest: they both dedicate themselves to hurting people they publicly profess to help.[16]

---

16 There are moral differences, though. Feminists support provoked abortion, which is an even uglier crime than fratricide, patricide, or their female versions. On the other hand, active pedophile priests severely reduce a kid's psychic stability and ability to love, which is, in my eyes, an even uglier crime than provoked abortion.

Hollywood and Feminism

This chapter starts out with a full quote of Manohla Dargis' foreword to the third edition[17] of Molly Haskell's 1974 classical book "From Reverence to Rape: the Treatment of Women in the Movies", as it gives an excellent "second wave feminist's appreciation" of the role of women in movies.[18]

> In 1974, the year that Molly Haskell's landmark "From Reverence to Rape: The Treatment of Women in the Movies" was first published, you had to squint to find a woman holding her own on the big screen. Typical of that year's higher-profile, more memorable female roles was Linda Blair's prepubescent girl who, in "The Exorcist", is possessed with a demonic strength that makes her head spin and wreaks havoc on her world. Unruly women, as Haskell illustrates in her wide-ranging book, have long been a cinematic staple alongside what she calls "the love goddesses, mothers, martyrs, spinsters, broads, virgins, vamps, prudes, adventuresses, she-devils, and sex kittens."
>
> More than forty years after its initial publication, "From Reverence to Rape" remains an essential volume for film specialists and generalists alike, a longevity that speaks to its breadth, depth, and significance. At once sweeping and detailed, historical and personal, the book traces the representation of women from the female-friendly silent era through Hollywood's by turns golden and corrosive ages and finally to the testosterone-fueled revolution of the 1970s known as New Hollywood. Few critics and theorists can move as effortlessly across eras—taking

---

17 The University of Chicago Press, 2016
18 Molly Haskell is primarily a movie criticist, and only secondarily a feminist, while Manohla Dargis the other way around

on different genres, stars, and directors—as Haskell does. She is as skilled discussing Frank Borzage's 1920s films with Janet Gaynor as she is writing about the new women's films of the early 1970s, in which the relegation of men to the shadows, she suggests, signals "a separation of the sexes more radical than at any previous point in our history." Haskell traced this gender divide back to the early 1960s, concluding that this period of social unrest had been "the most disheartening" in movie history. "In the roles and prominence accorded women," she writes, "the decade began unpromisingly, grew steadily worse, and at present shows no signs of improving." By 1987, for the second edition, she sounded a touch more optimistic, observing that "the treatment of women in the movies over the last ten years is the story of absence, followed by a fragmented, schizophrenic, but oddly hopeful presence." This fragmentation has remained a constant ever since. And, decades later, the separation of the sexes that Haskell diagnosed can feel like just another night at the movies, with men and women occupying entirely different screen worlds: comic-book superhero stories and cop movies and bromances, etc. for him — "chick flicks" for her.

To reread Haskell today is to understand that in "From Reverence to Rape" she wasn't only writing about cinema's past and present; she was also writing about the future that we now find ourselves in today. Because while much has changed for the better since 1974 —there are, for instance, more women directing movies than at any time in history— American mainstream cinema has for decades been dominated by movies about men for men and by men, from run-of-the-mill male-driven action pictures and animated children's movies to the superhero films that dominate annual box office charts

Hollywood and Feminism

with instructively named characters like Batman, Iron Man, Spider-Man, and Superman. Few of these movies offer leading roles for women, especially adults, which has resulted in a long-standing representational crisis in which female characters are radically marginalized and sometimes entirely absent.

"From Reverence to Rape" was published on the cusp of second-wave feminism, and its subject as well as its passion, which at times boils over into barely contained outrage, partly reflects its political moment (Some of Haskell's language, including her references to "man-haters" and "fag-hag," also reflect a certain period sensibility). That passion announces itself in the title of her first chapter, "The Big Lie," which she bracingly defines as "the idea of women's inferiority." Women thrived in cinema's earlier years, when the popularity of silent stars like Mary Pickford (who cofounded the film studio United Artists) helped justify the need for movies for and about women. Yet as the American movie industry developed into a big business, women were shut out from decision-making positions, including as directors. And this business, Haskell asserts in chapter after chapter, perpetuated the big lie.

Yet one of the great paradoxes of the movies —and perhaps its saving grace— is that even while women were being kept out of the studio front offices and the director's chair, the star system was producing immortals like of Pickford, Greta Garbo, Jean Harlow, Bette Davis, Katharine Hepburn, Barbara Stanwyck, Rosalind Russell, Joan Crawford, Grace Kelly, Audrey Hepburn, Doris Day, and Marilyn Monroe — and on and on and on. Women were shut out of the power corridors of an industry that they were helping to build, creating art and beauty, obscuring sexism and racism. Haskell is particularly brilliant on this contradiction, and shortly after introducing "the big lie" she presents some of the paradoxes that are familiar to those of us, women included, who love the movies even when they don't love us back: "the film industry maneuvered to keep women in their place; and yet these very myths and this machinery catapulted women into spheres of power beyond the wildest dreams of most of their sex."

The result was that even as women were excluded from both the production side and from the executive offices, the industry continued to speak to women audiences with female stars and female-driven stories. From the 1920s and through the 1930s, it was widely assumed in the industry that women were the principal consumers of movies, an assumption that helped build the star system and was instrumental in the development of so-called woman's pictures. By the 1950s, however, Hollywood — with findings from George Gallup's Audience Research Institute— had discovered the teenage market, a finding which, with the collapse of both the studio and star systems, proved calamitous for women. By the 1970s, the industry had decided that its target audience was male, a shift that at least one scholar suggests is the real marker of change between Hollywood's classical and postclassical periods. The movies did their part to perpetuate the big lie, including through the adoration and subjugation of women (the mother, the whore), who are put on pedestals only to be brutally, sometimes fatally knocked to the ground. Yet, as Haskell persuasively argues, certain performers, with their bigger-than life personalities and stardom, could complicate their roles exquisitely, as when Barbara Stanwyck turns a female stereotype like Stella Dallas into a multifaceted human being. Haskell's insistently dialectical approach is one reason why "From Reverence to Rape" is more complex than some of its detractors claimed, including some feminist film critics and theorists who, by the mid-1970s, had embraced Marx and Freud, Althusser and Lacan. Decades later, some of the criticisms of "Reverence to Rape" as reductively "image-based" themselves register as reductive and largely reflect the territorialism of film academics who, at the time, were polemically carving out a theoretical space of their own.

In her 1987 preface, Haskell identifies herself as "a film critic first and a feminist second." If she privileges movies over a political identity or ideological position it's because, as she wrote, she never wanted to "over-politicize the situation." Inherent in her declaration, of course, is that "the situation" —the representation of women in an industry historically dominated by men— is already political. In proclaiming herself a film critic first, Haskell isn't tempering her feminism; she is announcing the complexity of her project and also letting us know that while a critic must love her subject, she must never serve as its apologist. Film scholarship is filled with apologias, some better rationalized than others. The theorist Christian Metz wrote that to be a theoretician of the cinema, one should have "loved it a lot and only have detached oneself from it by taking it up again from the other end, taking it as the target for the very same scopic (sic) drive which had made one love it." For feminists, movie love can never be blind.

And "From Reverence to Rape" is a feminist history from the first page to the last, and a deeply personal one. In her introduction, Haskell weaves in asides from her own autobiography —as a woman, a southerner, film lover, film critic, and feminist— with a larger discussion of the actresses and types that she grew up watching, from the child performer Margaret O'Brien to the sexpots and nice girls of the 1950s. The references to sexpots and nice girls telegraphs Haskell's inductive approach: her book doesn't read as if it grew out of an existing theory or political allegiance but from a lifetime of watching movies — from collecting data, to put it another way. The index references more than 700 films from a wide range of genres that were produced over more than fifty years. Haskell poured a lifetime of loving movies into the book, but in setting her story against the larger one of women in movies she was declaring her allegiance to that familiar rallying cry of second-wave feminism: the personal is political.

Many years and theoretical polemics later the representational crisis that Haskell identified in "From Reverence to Rape" remains frustratingly with us. In 1942, the year that Bette Davis starred in "Now, Voyager", four out of the top nine movies at the American box office featured female stars who were billed above the title. When "The Hunger Games: Catching Fire", the second installment in the popular series with Jennifer Lawrence, became the highest grossing movie of 2013 it marked the first time that a movie with a lone female lead had topped the annual domestic box office since "The Exorcist" in 1973— forty years after Haskell finished her book! It's startling that the questions she posed at the end of her first edition remain relevant today. "How will women break through the barriers of a commercial cinema more truly monolithic in its sexism than it ever was in the old days of Hollywood? Where are the women to create new fictions, to go beyond the inner space— as women are doing every day in real life— into the outer world of invention, action, imagination?" Those of us who love movies know that the time for answers is now.

In the first paragraph of her foreword, Dargis mentions that in 1974, when Haskell wrote her classic book, which I will designate with the short "Reverence to Rape" from now on, women holding their own on the big screen were an exception. Rule were "unruly women, love goddesses, mothers, martyrs, spinsters, broads, virgins, vamps, prudes, adventuresses, she-devils, and sex kittens." Anno 2019 this has changed not only a lot, but quite over-the-top. Whereas the 1974 society was formed by women whose caricatures are given by the rule-list, in 2019 serious movies abound showing women showing off their "manly virtues", mostly reduced to combat skills. So if one may speak of a paradigm shift, this does not concern the nature of caricature (which is identically to the point for both sexes), but the creation of a new type of hero-out-of-nothing, the she-fighter. Little does it matter that those movies make me sometimes sick, sometimes laugh out loud; fact is that the avge American public takes those heroines seriously. Almost all police movies feature women as aggressive fighters. More and more non-police movies show the single-sense gender exchange. The lead role of "Salt" was originally offered to Tom Cruise film, but he turned it down. After that, Sony decided to go in a different direction by casting Angelina Jolie. Likewise, we have Jane Lynch, Sigourney Weaver, Jodie Foster, Helen Mirren, and Sandra Bullock; as far as Westerns are concerned, we have Lucy Liu, Viola Davis, Raquel Welch, Joan Crawford, Mercedes McCambridge, and Sharon Stone, to name just a few.

In Stone's least erotic movies she happily gallops around killing one bad fellow after the other. What is going on here? Apparently, Hollywood embraces its own kind of feminism: the one that degrades women to the role allotted them by a BC patriarchal society: women being subjugated by men, and even better, humiliating themselves of own accord.
Another issue feminists value highly is the number of female movie directors. Too bad, Dargis is too dumb to realize that only the yearly *ratios* of female to male directors are the important trend, not female absolute numbers.

In her first chapter, Haskell defines "The Big Lie" as "the idea of women's inferiority." According to Haskell, the Big Lie started when American movies developed into a big business, and this very business perpetuated the Big Lie. *Strangely, instead of simply calling sexism by its name,* Haskell turns to theoretical reasoning: "from the 1920s and through the 1930s, it was widely assumed in the industry that women were the principal consumers of movies, and that by the 1950s George Gallup's Audience Research Institute had discovered the teenage market, which proved calamitous for women because its target audience was male. Hence, the movies continued perpetuating the Big Lie, "including through the adoration and subjugation of women (the mother, the whore), who are put on pedestals only to be brutally, sometimes fatally knocked to the ground".

Well, apart from the facts she mentions, I believe her theory intended to "explain" female absence in directing roles is complete bull shit: a male teenage market? Never heard such nonsense before. This is a clear example of a male brain-washed female who thinks of herself as a feminist. Why would she mention the Gallup nonsense? She already gave the right reason, to wit, sexism. No need to add a digit more.

Upon carefully reading the final paragraph, Dargin's feminism crumbles down like a poorly built cathedral in stormy weathers. She compares the years 1942, 1973, and 2013, and exults upon realizing that, after the mute movie period (1942) in which female directors abounded, and a period of female elimination culminating in 1973, forty years after Haskell's book, finally comes the saving year 2013, which witnesses the first time that a movie with a lone female lead had topped the annual domestic box office since "The Exorcist" in 1973!

Well, my dear feminists, in my view this is Dargin's Big Lie: she hails an actress who mostly displays but a single virtue: that of male combat strength. This is feminism without a femininity. Hence, we are back at the beginning: what is the reason of this ever increasing sexism? Of course second-wave feminism will never agree, but it is my firm belief[19] that *this feminism failed, not due to poor performance of feminists, but due to EZ:[20] it requires women to submit to men, independently of women's intellectual virtues.* Just like in the Ancient Hebrew culture.

Note that this is not a characteristic of the ancient Hebrew culture only. It is a characteristic of all non-Catholic cultures. Take, as an example, the peoples belonging to the Eastern Semitic language group as shown in the graph

---

19   I have tried to underpin this belief in a 300-page thick book entitled "The Snake" (2019)
20   The owner of Hollywood, described in detail in the book mentioned in the previous footnote

below.[21] No doubt the complete Semitic tradition considers women as property, not only the Hebrews.

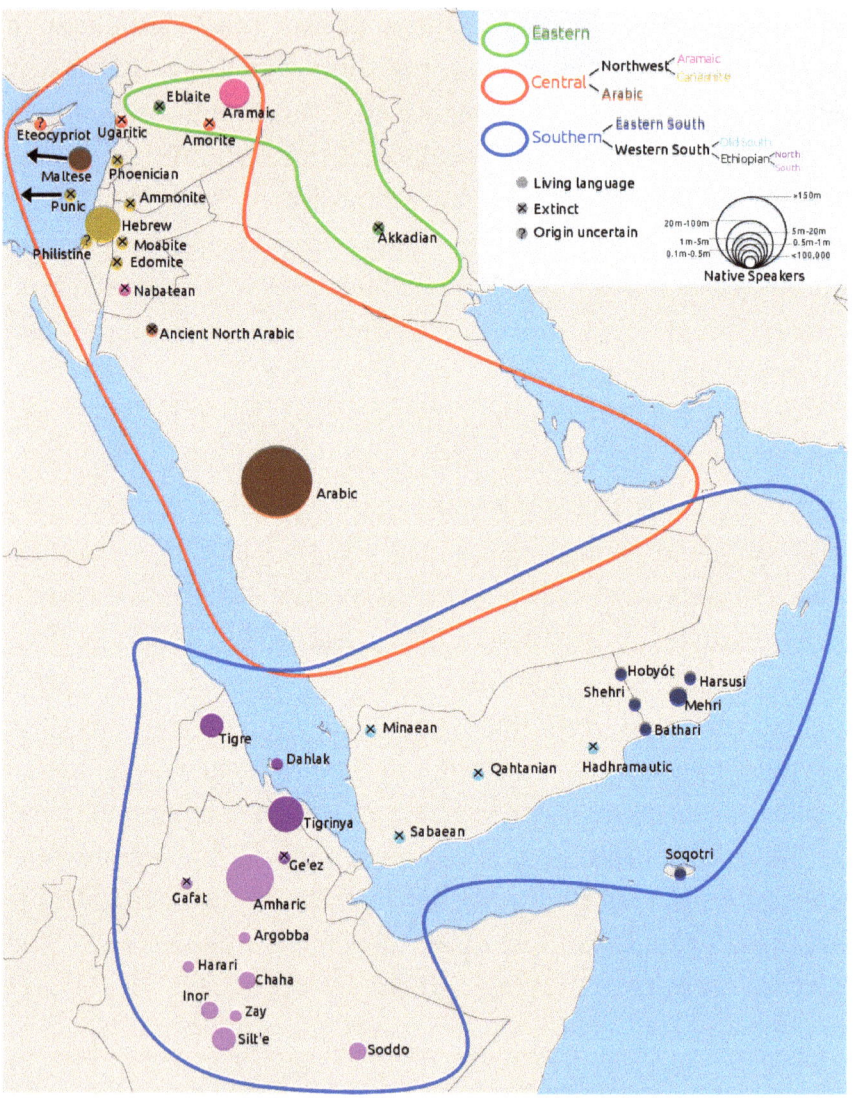

---

21 The Western Semitic language group contains fully Mali, Mauretania, Western Sahara, Tunisia, Libya, Egypt, and Sudan.

CHAPTER 4

Hollywood and Religion

4.1 Marah Eakin: a Movie Critic?

In February 2014, Marah Eakin wrote a typical Hollywood piece of criticism on *Robin Hood: Prince of Thieves*,[22] for AV/FILM, in the category "Memory Wipe". She smelled blood, and thought she knew how to get there. Below follows Marah Eakin's full text:[23]

23 years after its release, "Robin Hood: Prince of Thieves" is barely watchable: by Marah Eakin[24]

My family owned about three movies when I was growing up. We were a library clan; if we wanted to watch something, we'd either pick it up or order it from the Cuyahoga County Public Library, a system that worked

---

22 Featuring Kevin Costner, Alan Rickman, Mary Elizabeth Mastrantonio, and Morgan Freeman; released in 1991; directed by Kevin Reynolds; written by Pen Densham and John Watson; and produced by Warner Brothers.
23 https://film.avclub.com/23-years-after-its-release-robin-hood-prince-of-thiev-1798272872
24 10/02/14 in AV/FILM, category MEMORY WIPE.

most of the time. But for whatever reason, we actually owned hard copies of a few things. One was *Fantasia*, which I've still never watched. Another was a dubbed copy of *Amadeus* that one of my parents' friends must have given them. (Again, haven't watched it, though I should.) And the third was a real, honest-to-goodness store-bought copy of *Robin Hood: Prince Of Thieves*.

I have no idea where that copy of *Robin Hood* came from—a friend of my parents' as a gift to us kids, maybe?—but seeing as how it was the only movie in the house that both my brother and I agreed on at any given time, I must have watched that tape 100 times. I haven't seen it in at least 20 years, but I can still recite portions of it backward and forward ("No blades, no bows. Leave your weapons here."), and (until recently) I remembered it fondly, thinking wistfully of a heroic Kevin Costner sweeping his Maid Marian around on a rope.

Like so much media from our collective youths, though, *Robin Hood: Prince Of Thieves* doesn't hold up. Twenty-three years after its theatrical release, revisiting the film is a positively painful experience, especially in the almost three-hour director's cut available to stream via Amazon. *Thieves* is a clunky, poorly acted movie arguably intended for adults but embraced by kids who just didn't know better. (Though the existence of an extensive Kenner line of *Prince Of Thieves* action figures suggests the toymaker knew kids were going to like it from the get-go.) It's confoundingly disjointed, sweepingly racist and sexist, and full of both bad costumes and bad wigs.

Though I remembered him as this devil-may-care rake with a swath of luxurious hair, Costner's Robin is both poorly styled and wildly inconsistent as a character, not just because of Costner's barely existent British accent, but because Robin apparently both achieves and loses adult sensibilities over the course of the film. He's willing to sacrifice his hand to save a friend at the beginning of the movie, but, once returned to England, he acts like a petulant child, teasing his new friend Azeem about love. And though it seems noble that he eventually decides to take up with a band of outlaws and overthrow the corrupt sheriff, the film doesn't actually explain *why* he'd do that, other than to imply that it was just the right thing to do. Mary Elizabeth Mastrantonio's Marian is similarly wishy-washy, entering the film as a strong woman who's skilled with a sword and exiting it as a lady barely capable of defending herself against an old witch's prying claws. Speaking of Maid Marian and the film's romantic element, *woof*. Though 12th-century England certainly didn't lend itself to lengthy love stories or even ideal matches, the fact that Marian would fall head over heels in L-O-V-E love with Robin after seeing his pale, naked ass through a waterfall, well, it's comical at best. Sure, she may have fallen in lust, but the film lets the camera linger on Mastrantonio's gaping face in the scene, suggesting that, as if struck by Cupid's arrow, she's simply fallen for a guy she barely knows. And while this trope isn't uncommon in films or in fiction in general, it's just another example of how *Prince Of Thieves*' plot is spotty at best, relying on viewers to already know the story and fill in the gaps themselves.

Much has been made—rightfully so—of the film's treatment of Morgan Freeman's Azeem character, the Moor that escapes a Jerusalem jail with Robin and is summarily indebted to him by decree of Allah. While the film's dialogue certainly does Azeem no favors, calling him "the painted man" and making a joke out of his faith a few times, *Robin Hood: Prince Of Thieves* still mostly contains a message about acceptance of others, with

Freeman's Azeem overall reading as a clever, loyal, and learned man. (Costner's ham-fisted speech to the Merry Men about color and creed, though? Ugh. He should never be counted on to deliver long blocks of "sincere" dialogue.)

The film doesn't handle paganism as well, with both Alan Rickman's sheriff and his witch mother Mortianna stumbling comically around runes, pentagrams, and dry-ice steam baths. Mortianna is especially ridiculous, with British actress Geraldine McEwan clad in a thin, balding gray wig, oddly colored contacts, and one really long fingernail, which she drags across a metal tray at one point, making a noise that turns my stomach to this day. She's meant to be this hideous, devious witch, and while McEwan arguably plays that role well, it's so ridiculously over the top and comical that she practically becomes a Disney character, albeit one with a penchant for spit and blood.

Mortianna also features prominently the film's lengthy and uncomfortable attempted-rape scene. While I remembered this scene from watching the movie growing up, I don't remember it being *so* horrifying, as well as so comically played. Rickman's sheriff is pushy and jovial as he forces Marian's legs apart, and while his jokes about how hard it is for him to get, well, hard, are probably supposed to be funny, 23 years and a world of political correctness later, they just seem cruel. Other aspects of the rape scene are—understandably—just disgusting. In particular, Mortianna's claim that Marian is "ripe" and "will bear a son" after touching her stomach is hideously crass and downright icky, on top of being (along with the actual rape, for crying out loud) utterly and completely inappropriate for the movie's PG-13 viewers.

And that really underscores the movie's biggest problem.

Watching the movie in a society 23 years more advanced, both technologically and culturally, I found myself wondering just who *Robin Hood: Prince Of Thieves* was for in the first place. If the experiences of my friends, loved ones, and coworkers are any indication, it was meant for kids with a taste for action and explosions with few scruples about either acting or dialogue. But given the movie's cast—Costner, Rickman, Freeman, Mastrantonio, Christian Slater, and a brief appearance from Sean Connery—it seems like the filmmakers and producers at least tried to approach the story with some seriousness. Certain characters, like Mike McShane's Friar Tuck, are no doubt meant to add levity to the hand-chopping and macabre production. But others, like Rickman's sheriff, sweep so wildly from horrifically serious to ridiculously comical that it seems like, halfway through the production, the cast and director just said, "Fuck it. Let's have a little fun with this one." And while that's the kind of stuff that makes a movie memorable to a 10-year-old me—particularly when you don't question how whole treehouse villages are built overnight in the forest without anyone in Nottingham's employ noticing—it's also the kind of stuff that makes a movie damn near unwatchable for a 33-year-old me. Despite what I thought 23 years ago, whimsy and costuming only go so far toward creating a great movie. Black powder and Christian Slater are cool and all, but real dramatic successes come when a film has both heart *and* a slate of talented actors who aren't just leaning on their oversized patchwork capes to tell the story.

4.2 Marah Eakin? Alas, Just a Cheap Mercenary

Marah Eakin mentions some incongruities in the libretto, the disjointed, racist and sexist character of the movie, Marian falling in love with Robin after seeing his naked ass through a waterfall, and the profound disgust provoked by the Sheriff's rape attempt, while his mother Mortianna plays the witch. A disjointed movie? Not as disjointed as her own criticism: in a single sentence she manages to say tha "Mortianna's fingernail scratch on a metal surface *makes your stomach turn to this day*", while qualifying her role as "so ridiculously over the top and comical that she practically becomes a Disney character".[25]

Her whole story does not sound like movie criticism. It rather seems an adult's surprise upon revisiting her minuscule kindergarten which she always had thought of as a huge castle with lots of surprises and hiding places.[26]

---

[25] Apparently Disney characters are able to turn her stomach to this day. Quite understandable, as her main ideological dogma holds that cultural advance is equal to technological advance. This dogma is wrong, and there are enough examples for the readership to see that: just think of the fall of the two Roman Empires, which set back the cultural clock by a full century for the people involved.

[26] Furthermore, she gives the childish impression of ignoring the nature of a rape. There are so many movies illustrating realistic rapes that it is actually hard to believe a professional movie critic never saw one. Does she really mistake a real rape for a symbolized attempt. I blush to mention this, but the whole rape scene is obviously meant comically, with Azeem attempting to break open the door. The audience does not even get to see Mastrantonio's ankles! In a realistic rape, dear Marah, the victim is usually first

Third, does she really think that Marian fell in love upon seeing Robin naked at the waterfall? Doesn't she mistake love for sex, poor Marah? Or has Hollywood totally blunted what little was left of her ideas of romance? What is she, Marah, a badly programmed computer?

A tiny spark of romanticism suffices to locate Marian's falling in love at her first encounter with adult Robin, "that nasty boy that used to burn her hair for fun". The mere fact that Marian complains about it to Robin is a silent cry for intimate apologies; it represents a candid exposure of her vulnerability, too.[27] And finally, what about Marian's facial and bodily gestures, when Robin steals her horses, that *normal women* (ab)use when they love a man? Amazing that Marah missed these details[28] all the 100 times she claims to have seen the movie. As far as the director is concerned, Marah complains about how the movie deals with paganism.[29] However, she fails to mention the satire on

---

    heavily hit to reduce her defensive power, and to induce her to submit without further defense attempts. Next her clothes are torn off her body, and then a rather plain phenomenon occurs which is called *penetration*. Am I really explaining this to you, Marah? Where is the man's hitting, the victim's blooding, and the victim's nudity in *Prince of Thieves*? Marian wears an intact robe down to her ankles during the whole rape scene, by Jupiter!

27 That is called a "romantic advance", for all the Marah's that did not get it, used as they are to overt sexual advances. The latter are but shameful signs of absence of both education and culture.

28 like lying about Azeem and Robin stealing her horses

29 Marah about ridiculing religions: "The film doesn't handle paganism as well, with both Alan Rickman's sheriff and his witch mother Mortianna stumbling comically around runes, pentagrams, and dry-ice steam baths." So how would Marah propose to ridicule Paganism?

Catholicism (brother Tuck) that of Islam (English clouds), and most importantly, that of Judaism. What exactly were those hoodies doing, mumbling around a huge map of England, when suddenly the sheriff of Nottingham (impersonated by an excellently performing Rickman) jumps in and proposes a deal he is not even able to hold up? *Would that not be a satire of Zionism?* How come Marah forgot to mention that one?30

Kevin Costner, in his excellent interpretation of Robin Hood in "The Prince of Thieves".

---

30 Was it part of the instructions she got? Remark, she wrote her severe critique in 2014, exactly halfway the 2010 edition (with Russel Crowe) and the 2018 one (with Taron Egerton). Is that by chance, or again part of the instructions? The latter are two standard Hollywood productions, in spite of all actor quality investment. Compare Crowe's Robin Hood to his Gladiator, and the former vanishes. The only political difference with Prince of Thieves is that the 2014 and 2018 Robin Hoods do not contain the least reference to Judaism, while still allowing puns on Christianity and Islam.

APPENDIX

Rotten-Tomatoes Appreciation of Cahiers-elected Movies

A1.1 Top 10 Movies of *Cahiers du Cinéma*

Wikipedia presents the annual top 10 lists from the *Cahiers du Cinéma*. Because there is way too much information in these lists, I compiled decade overviews based on those annual lists. Because the Cahiers are French, I chose to put but two French movies in the self-compiled lists, in order to correct, to first order, for French patriotism. Nothing wrong with the latter, of course. The fact that the French started these Cahiers obviously implies they were the first to professionally discuss movies, which on its own turn implies that the French were the first professional movie makers. I hope the French forgive me for this way of proceeding. Below is the result of my Cahier-based compilation, for the last four decades.

1980-1989	Director
Francisca	Manoel de Oliveira
The Aviator's Wife	Éric Rohmer
Merry Christmas	Nagisa Oshima
Class Relations	Straub & Huillet
Year of the Dragon	Michael Cimino
Legend of Suram Fortress	Sergei Parajanov
The Death of Empedocles	Straub & Huillet
A Short Film About Killing	Krzysztof Kieślowski
Red Wood Pigeon	Nanni Moretti

1990 – 1999	Director
The Bridges of Madison Cy	Clint Eastwood
Carlito's Way	Brian De Palma
Goodbye South, Goodbye	Hou Hsiao-hsien
Up-Close & Personal	Abbas Kiarostami
Eyes Wide Shut	Stanley Kubrick
Twin Peaks	David Lynch
Unforgiven	Clint Eastwood
Crash	David Cronenberg
Edward Scissorhands	Tim Burton

Appreciation 39

2000 – 2009	Director
Mulholland Drive	David Lynch
Elephant	Gus Van Sant
Tropical Malady	Weerasethakul
The Host	Bong Joon-ho
A History of Violence	David Cronenberg
The Secret of the Grain	Abdellatif Kechiche
War of the Worlds	Steven Spielberg
The New World	Terrence Malick
Ten	Abbas Kiarostami

2010-2018	Director
Uncle Boonmee…	Weerasethakul
We Have a Pope	Nanni Moretti
Cosmopolis	David Cronenberg
Spring Breakers	Harmony Korine
Under the Skin	Jonathan Glazer
Toni Erdmann	Maren Ade
Phantom Thread	Paul Anderson

A1.2 Hollywood Trends

The list of Rotten-Tomatoes criticism on *Cahiers*-elected movies (see appendix) evidence some important trends.
First, The election committee of *Cahiers du Cinéma* sits in an ivory tower, where it cultivates some insider's ideology which nobody is interested to know, and manages, more effectively as years go by, the elect movies which score lowest

with the public. If *Cahiers* wants to *communicate at all*, they should at least leave that ivory tower momentarily, while humiliating themselves to the unthinkable deep level of making their ideology public and open for discussion. If they wait another decade with doing so, the *Cahiers du Cinéma* will turn into a fossil.

Second, *Rotten Tomatoes* itself is performing worse with time, too, although not quite as bad as *Cahiers du Cinéma*. Their predictions are systematically too high, and, especially for the weaker movies, they sometimes manage to predict twice the public's rating. Two decades more, and *Rotten Tomatoes* can award a Rotten Tomato to itself.

Third, the *Cahiers*-elected movies are Hollywoodizing at such a pace that they are close to saturation. During the 1980's and 1990's, the *Cahiers*-elected movies (and I believe, the movies in general) were not as laden with violence and sexual deviations. Quite to the contrary, the latter seem to be the main features of the *Cahiers*-elected movies of the 2000's and 2010's. The only exceptions are Asian movies, whose directors are not as sex-addicted as European and US directors. Violence there is a lot too, in Asian movies, although it is more stylized and meditated: in Japanese movies, people fly through the air with totally unrealistic jumps, or they beat the enemy by the concentration of prayer, meditation, or however one likes to call it.

On the other hand, Bollywood always shows happy faces of actors in love, trying to bridge the Indian Caste system in order to reach their beloved. Chinese movies reveal the hardships of communism, and usually present virtuous main characters whose intention is to help out poor people: those country-people that the Chinese government has been trying to get rid of in the last two decades, by means of their immoral single-child law.

Hollywood, instead, shows angry, frustrated faces, in search for vengeance, only to find out that vengeance does not yield personal satisfaction; or it shows anguished faces, of people finding themselves in extremely awkward circumstances, usually due to blackmail by mafias.

A1.3 Prophetical Nature of Dystopias

The strangest aspect of Hollywood is that its many movies on slavery and vexation (e.g. The Hunger Games, 2012, starring Jennifer Lawrence, directed by Gary Ross, based on Suzanne Collins' dystopia) are really prophetic: Big Brother (all-powerful in Hollywood and in all trend-setting international news media, in the US Ministry of Defense, and in US international policy) is preparing our mind-set, that of the future slaves in Big Brother's New World Order. Everybody sympathizes with the heroin, district-girl Katniss Everdeen (Jennifer Lawrence), and nobody with the Capitol's President Snow (Donald Sutherland), don't we? Some decades more of this kind of brain-washing, and we, the district slaves, will happily accept our new roles in the New world Order, so kindly offered to us by Big Bro.

A1.4 The Morality of Movies

In the course of time, movies have quite altered their moral or psychological-impact ratings. The table below shows the four categories used in the US.

The MPAA-category "X" was introduced in 1968, cautioning for nudity and profanity, read "almost pornographic". The honor of the creation of this special dirt category was all director's Brian De Palma (Robert de Niro's debut film). A clean-up of the movie allowed it to be reduced to R.

Rating	Audience
G (General)	all ages admitted
Parental Guidance	not for children
PG-13	not for children<13
R (Restricted)	== PG-17
NC (Not for Children)	above 17 only
NR (Non-rated)	for TV

Non-rated or unrated movies are those that have not been submitted to the *Motion Picture Association of America* (MPAA) yet. *ThoughtCo* explains:[31]

> The first attempts at censoring movies were made by cities, not the film industry. Chicago and New York City in the early 1900s both gave police the authority to determine what could and could not be shown. And in 1915, the U.S. Supreme Court ruled that movies were not considered protected speech under the First Amendment and thus were subject to regulation.
> In response, leading movie studios formed the Motion Picture Producers and Distributors of America (MPPDA),

---

31 https://www.thoughtco.com/how-does-a-movie-get-its-rating-2423408

Appreciation

> an industry lobbying organization, in 1922. To head the organization, the MPPDA hired former postmaster general William Hays. Hays didn't just lobby politicians on behalf of filmmakers; he also told the studios what was and was not considered acceptable content.
>
> Throughout the 1920s, filmmakers grew bolder with their choice of subject matter. By today's standards, the occasional glimpse of a bare leg or a suggestive word seems tame, but in that era such behavior was scandalous. Films like "The Wild Party" (1929) with Clara Bow and "She Done Him Wrong" (1933) with Mae West titillated viewers and infuriated social conservatives and religious leaders.

The last paragraph is of extreme importance. In the 1930's the mere voluntary, intentional flirt of a woman showing her bare leg was considered scandalous. Today, American adults do not even blink when movies are released that show nudity for mere erotic purposes, sometimes two full hours long. I could not care less about such a societal change,[32] weren't it that the sexual liberation promoted by movie lobbyists seems to be the very cause that women were treated as ladies in the 1930's, while as potential whores toward the end of the 2010's.

ThoughtCo continues its historical account:

> In 1930, Hays unveiled his Motion Picture Production Code, which soon came to be known as the Hays Code. Its mission was to ensure that the movies depicted "correct standards of life" and, studio executives hoped, to avoid

---

[32] Apart for research purposes, as it happened so fast, with a still increasing growth rate

the future threat of government censorship. But MPPDA officials struggled to keep up with Hollywood's output, and the Hays Code was largely ineffectual for its first years.

That changed in 1934 when Hays hired Joseph I. Breen, a lobbyist with deep ties to the Catholic Church, to head the new Production Code Administration. Going forward, every film had to be reviewed and rated to be released. Breen and his team took to their work with zest. For example, "Casablanca" (1942) had its famous ending scene altered to tone down the sexual tension between Humphrey Bogart's and Ingrid Bergman's characters.

In the 1940s, a handful of filmmakers circumvented Hollywood censors by releasing their films independently of the studio system. Most notable was "The Outlaw," a 1941 film starring Jane Russell that gave ample screen time to her famous bosom. After battling censors for five years, director Howard Hughes finally persuaded United Artists to release the film, which was a box office smash. Breen tightened the code's restrictions in 1951, but its days were numbered.

While some liturgy-nuts of the Catholic Church were busying themselves with excommunicating half a millennium of Roman liturgy,[33] and while others produced lengthy

---

33   Since the Council of Trent, which occurred 1545-1563, the Catholic Church had been using a single Roman liturgy throughout the world (among all accepted liturgies). The two Vatican Councils (1869-1870 and 1962-1965) not only reformed the Roman liturgy (which can be good or bad, depending on the changes proposed), but the liturgists were so excessively intolerant and self-conceited (as never seen in Church history before) that they simply *banned* the Tridentine liturgy, for being (in their view) totally unfit for the

Appreciation 45

theoretical criticisms on rationalism, liberalism, and materialism, they completely forgot to address the *practical* issues. I am not aware of any decree dating from 1934 (when Hays hired Joseph Breen), concerning the possible ways in which Catholics could fight the degradation of women in movies and on TV. *ThoughtCo* continues:

> Hollywood continued to abide by the Motion Picture Production Code into the early 1960s. But as the old studio system crumbled and cultural tastes changed, Hollywood realized that it needed a new way to rate films. In 1968, the Motion Picture Association of America (MPAA), the successor to the MPPDA, created the MPAA Ratings System.
> Initially, the system had four grades: G (general audiences), M (mature), R (restricted), and X (explicit). However, the MPAA never trademarked the X rating, and what was intended for legitimate films soon was co-opted by the pornography industry, which outdid itself to advertise films rated with a single, double, or even triple X.
> The system was overhauled repeatedly over the years. In 1972, the M rating was changed to PG. Twelve years later, the violence in "Indiana Jones and the Temple of Doom" 300 and "Gremlins," both of which had received a PG rating, prompted the MPCC to create the PG-13 rating. In 1990, the MPAA unveiled the NC-17 rating,

---

twentieth century. I still need to meet the first liturgist who can argue why a liturgy that was apparently fit during 400 years, was not complemented with simplified liturgies, but bluntly put aside as something evil or heretical. Not right in their minds, these liturgists.

intended for mainstream films like "Henry and June" and "Requiem for a Dream."

Kirby Dick, whose documentary "This Film Is Not Yet Rated" (2006) examines the history of the MPAA, has criticized the ratings for being too subjective, particularly with depictions of sex and violence. For its part, the MPAA is trying to be more detailed about what the ratings are for. Phrases like "Rated PG-13 for science-fiction violence" now appear in the ratings, and the MPAA has begun offering more details on the rating process on its website.

The history described by *ThoughtCo* shows an interesting fight between the families wanting to protect their children on one side, and the XXX psycho-nuts, pedophiles, and violent sex maniacs on the other. Most of the fights are men's, however. It is not a bad thing that men fight for their rights, but women have a different perspective on many things, and their role in this fight is as necessary as that of men.

In the remainder of this appendix, I reproduce Rotten Tomatoes' description of *Cahiers'* highest-ranked movies.

A1.5 *Cahiers'* rankings with *Rotten's* Comments

Francisca (1981) by Manoel de Oliveira

Avge Tomato vs Watcher's Rating: 72%-78%
Manoel de Oliveira wrote and directed this historical drama about the lives of some of his wife's ancestors who were active in the first half of the 19th century. In order to put across this slower-paced era before automobiles, planes, instant television and radio news, and computers, Oliveira uses a series of tableaus to emphasize the drama of each setting and the lifestyle of the protagonists. The feckless, wealthy Jose Augusto (Diogo Doria) and Fanny Owen (Teresa Meneses), a young

English woman, are attracted to each other. A perennial love triangle is created when the author Camilo Castelo Branco (Mario Barroso) also falls in love with Fanny (Francisca), but is placed in a bind because he is a friend of Jose Augusto. In the end Fanny opts for the wealthy young man, and Camilo (who would eventually die by suicide) loses the love of his life. Now that the rich young man has succeeded in the chase, he has no interest in the result, and he and Fanny are married by proxy. Although she goes to live in his mansion, he does not stay with her and she is left alone — and untouched. The triangle has come apart, and Fanny and Camilo have been separated, almost by the whim of the rich and disinterested Jose Augusto. ~ Eleanor Mannikka, Rovi

The Aviator's Wife (1981) by Éric Rohmer

Avge Tomato vs Watcher's Rating: 73%-83%
Fresh-Rotten Reviews: 8-0
François, a young student working nights as a postman, is in love with a slightly older woman, Anne. One day, he sees Anne's former lover, a pilot named Christian, leaving Anne's apartment in the morning. Despite Anne's explanation that Christian is now married to another woman and simply dropped by to talk, François becomes jealous. He starts spying on Christian in order to find out if his rival secretly sees Anne. Though François sees Christian meeting a different woman, he keeps following the pair. His pursuit leads him to a park where he meets up with a vivacious teenage girl named Lucie, who becomes curious about his motives and agrees to help him in his detection. ~ Yuri German, Rovi

Merry Christmas, Mr. Lawrence (1983) by Nagisa Oshima

Avge Tomato vs Watcher's Rating: 80%-79%
Fresh-Rotten Reviews: 16-4
This movie was the first English-language project of Japanese director Nagisa Oshima (Death by Hanging, In the Realm of the Senses). In tune with his previous filmic essays on racism and brutality, Merry Christmas concentrates on a war of wills between rebellious POW Major Jack Celliers (David Bowie) and camp commandant Captain Yonoi (Ryuichi Sakomoto). Assuming that his other prisoners' unwillingness to protest their cruel treatment is a sign of weakness, Yonoi is most impressed by Celliers' enigmatic defiance. While Celliers and Yonoi seem to be operating on a high spiritual and intellectual plane, bilingual prisoner Colonel John Lawrence (Tom Conti) engages in a more standard adversarial relationship with sadistic Sergeant Gengo Hara.

Class Relations (1984)
by Jean Straub & Danièle Huillet

Avge Watcher's Rating: 65%

Financed in Germany and filmed in New York, Class Relations is adapted from Franz Kafka's unfinished novel Amerika. Christian Heinisch plays a bourgeois German forced to leave his homeland after a scandal. He accepts his uncle's invitation to move to America, where he takes a succession of "Joe Jobs." Heinisch tries, but he is unable to shake off his old-world customs. Worse, the class structure in Europe never prepared him to have to actually use his hands to make a living. Rather than tack on an ending of their own, writer/directors Danièle Huillet and Jean-Marie Straub conclude Class Relations in the same manner that Kafka left Amerika behind when he died--with the hero's ultimate fate still in limbo.

Year of the Dragon (1985) by Michael Cimino

Avge Tomato vs Watcher's Rating: 59%-52%
Fresh-Rotten Reviews: 10-7
Best known for his 1978 film The Deer Hunter or perhaps the less-successful Heaven's Gate, director Michael Cimino turned to this fast-paced actioner set in an authentic (back lot) Chinatown. This thriller stars a rogue Polish-American cop (Mickey Rourke) out to not only keep Chinatown safe for the local consumers, but to dismantle its deep-rooted crime and drug cartels as well. No one backs the crusading cop in the latter objective, and as he faces a suave and wily crime boss (John Lone of The Last Emperor) and a libidinous newscaster (Ariane), he may be taking on more than he can handle. At least his wife thinks so, and the guys at City Hall think so -- but mayhem and murder will strew the streets with corpses before the smoke clears and the dust settles, and a vague, unresolved future sets in. ~ Eleanor Mannikka, Rovi

Appreciation 53

Legend of Suram Fortress (1986) by Sergei Paradzhanov

Avge Tomato vs Watcher's Rating: 75%-81%
Fresh-Rotten Reviews: 6-2
Directors Paradzhanov and Abashidze resurrected an old Soviet Georgian folktale as the basis for their film The Legend of Suram Fortress. The fortress in question is forever under construction, and forever collapsing before the last brick can be laid. The advice of a fortuneteller is sought out; the young fellow sent out to seek this advice hap-pens to be the son of a man who years earlier had jilted the fortuneteller. Out of pique, she tells him that he must be walled up in the fortress' wall, else the structure will continue to tumble. So many ancient legends are based upon self-sacrifice that one would think that Legend of Suram Fortress would have nothing new to offer. Never as brilliant as the critics made it out to be, Suram Fortress is still an immensely satisfying work from a gifted filmmaking team.

The Death of Empedocles (1987) by Huillet and Straub

Noted modernist German filmmakers Danièle Huillet and Jean-Marie Straub are behind this evocative minimalist retelling of the tragic story of Empedocles, a Greek philosopher and statesman who lived in the fourth century BC. To prove himself a god and therefore, immortal, Empedocles hurled himself into the burning caldera of Mount Etna and survived. There are four slightly different versions of the film available.

Appreciation

A Short Film About Killing (1988) by Krzysztof Kieślowski

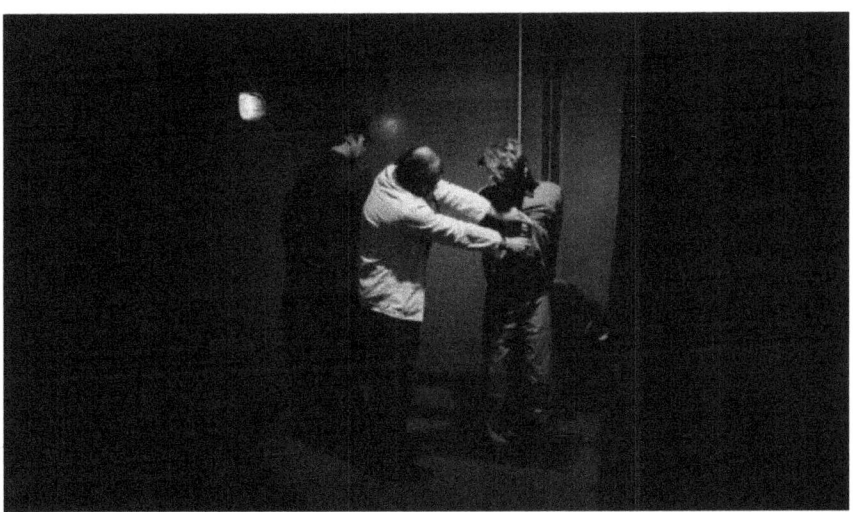

Avge Tomato vs Watcher: 90%-90%
Fresh-Rotten Reviews: 19-2
This disturbing and violent feature opens with a scene of a dead rat and a lifeless cat hanging by the neck. As the plot unfolds, Yatzek (Miroslaw Baka) is a 20-year-old drifter who murders a testy taxi driver (Jan Tesarz) in a gut-wrenching scene of excessive violence. Tension continues to build as a newly licensed young attorney (Krzysztof Globisz is chosen to represent Yatzek in court. Much anticipated and well-received at Cannes, the film won the European Film Academy Award for "Best European Film" in 1988.

Edward Scissorhands (1990) by Tim Burton

Avge Tomato vs Watcher's Rating: 90%-91%
Fresh-Rotten Reviews: 52-6

Tim Burton's Edward Scissorhands opens as an eccentric inventor (Vincent Price) lovingly assembles a synthetic youth named Edward (Johnny Depp). Edward has all the essential ingredients for today's standard body, with the exception of a pair of hands. For what is initially thought to be a temporary period, he is fitted with long, scissor-like extremities that, while able to trim a mean hedge, are hardly conducive to day-to-day life. When the kindly inventor dies, however, Edward is left lonely and cursed with some very heavy metal for hands. He is eventually taken in by Peg Boggs (Dianne Weist), an Avon lady who takes pity on him after seeing his bleak existence. Edward, in spite of his inherent ability to slay anyone he comes across, is a gentle soul whose only wish is to be loved. ~ Tracie Cooper, Rovi

Appreciation

Twin Peaks (1992) by David Lynch

Avge Tomato vs Watcher's Rating: 63%-78%
Fresh-Rotten Reviews: 46-27

This dark drama is the prequel to the TV series, Twin Peaks, also by director David Lynch. A woman who seems to be innocent and pure by day leads a double life in a rural community where quite a bit of evil lurks just beneath the surface of an otherwise typical American small town. As she was sexually abused throughout her childhood by her possessed father, Laura has some obvious sexual problems and is heavily addicted to cocaine. This film tells of the bizarre and twisted circumstances that led to her murder--which was where the television series began.

Unforgiven (1992) by Clint Eastwood

Avge Tomato vs Watcher's Rating: 96%-93%
Fresh-Rotten Reviews: 92-4
Dedicated to his mentors Sergio Leone and Don Siegel, Clint Eastwood's 1992 Oscar-winner examines the mythic violence of the Western, taking on the ghosts of his own star past. Disgusted by Sheriff "Little Bill" Daggett's decree that several ponies make up for a cowhand's slashing a whore's face, Big Whiskey prostitutes, led by fierce Strawberry Alice (Frances Fisher), take justice into their own hands and put a $1000 bounty on the lives of the perpetrators. Notorious outlaw-turned-hog farmer William Munny (Eastwood) is sought out by neophyte gunslinger the Schofield Kid (Jaimz Woolvett) to go with him to Big Whiskey and collect the bounty. While Munny insists, "I ain't like that no more," he needs the bounty money for his children, and the two men convince Munny's clean-living comrade Ned Logan (Morgan Freeman) to join them in righting a wrong done to a woman. Little Bill (Oscar-

winner Gene Hackman), however, has no intention of letting any bounty hunters impinge on his iron-clad authority. When pompous gunman English Bob (Richard Harris) arrives in Big Whiskey with pulp biographer W.W. Beauchamp (Saul Rubinek) in tow, Little Bill beats Bob senseless and promises to tell Beauchamp the real story about violent frontier life and justice. But when Munny, the true unwritten legend, comes to town, everyone soon learns a harsh lesson about the price of vindictive bloodshed and the malleability of ideas like "justice." "I don't deserve this," pleads Little Bill. "Deserve's got nothin' to do with it," growls Munny, simultaneously summing up the insanity of western violence and the legacy of Eastwood's Man With No Name. ~ Lucia Bozzola, Rovi

Carlito's Way (1993) by Brian De Palma

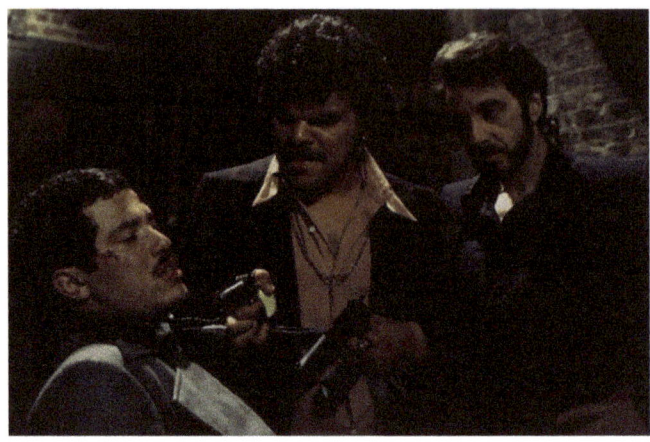

Avge Tomato vs Watcher's Rating: 80%-91%
Fresh-Rotten Reviews: 37-9

Carlito's Way is a tale of a former hood trying to escape his former life. Al Pacino is Carlito Brigante, a high-level Puerto Rican drug dealer sprung from a three-decade jail sentence after only five years, thanks to a technicality and his sleazy, cocaine-addled lawyer, Dave Kleinfeld (Sean Penn). Carlito renounces his previous ways and takes a job as the manager of a club that Kleinfeld has invested in, planning to save enough money so that he can eventually move to the Caribbean. But no sooner is Carlito back on the streets of New York than his old life claws at him in the form of both old partners (Luis Guzman) and vicious up-and-comers (John Leguizamo). Nevertheless, Carlito stays clean and even restarts his relationship with a dancer named Gail (Penelope Ann Miller), until he is finally led astray by Kleinfeld, who manipulates Carlito into participating in the murder of a Mafia don from whom Kleinfeld has stolen a million dollars.

Appreciation

The Bridges of Madison County (1995) by Clint Eastwood

Avge Tomato vs Watcher's Rating: 90%-87%
Fresh-Rotten Reviews: 52-6
The brief, illicit love affair between an Iowa housewife and a post-middle-age free-lance photographer is chronicled in this powerful romance based on the best-selling novella by Robert James Waller. The story begins as globetrotting National Geographic photographer Robert Kincaid journeys to Madison County in 1965 to film its lovely covered bridges. Upon his arrival, he stops by an old farmhouse to ask directions. There he encounters housewife, Francesca Johnson, whose spouse and two children are out of town. Thus begins their four-day affair, a liaison that fundamentally changes them both. Later Francesca chronicles the affair in a diary which her flabbergasted grown children read; never would they have expected their mother to be capable of the passion she experienced with Kincaid. ~ Sandra Brennan, Rovi

Goodbye South, Goodbye (1996) by Hou Hsiao-hsien

Avge Watcher's Rating: 87%

Produced by the Japanese Shochiku Company, this Taiwanese drama follows the lives of two generations of Taipei residents. Kao is a gangster, while divorcee/single mother/bar hostess Ying is his girlfriend.

Kao's closest friend is rock singer Flathead and his slightly ditzy girlfriend Pretzel. The troubles begin when Kao and his long-time cohort Hsi and the others set up a temporary gambling den in the highlands.

As the day progresses, Pretzel gets so deeply into debt that she attempts suicide. Later Kao and His get some bad news about a shady business venture in Shanghai. To make some quick money, His and Kao devise a new scam to get the government to condemn so land so the two can quickly buy up all the pigs upon it and then sell them to their fellow gangsters, to the government and to the local farmers. The plan works until Flathead decides to flex his muscles and get some of his relatives, who live in the air, to pay their debts.

Close-Up (1996) by Abbas Kiarostami

Avge Tomato vs Watcher's Rating: 31%-66%
Fresh-Rotten Reviews: 24-11
A story about a career television journalist who eclipses her mentor, this drama's plot resembles that of A Star Is Born, and it shares the same screenwriters as those who penned the 1976 version of that film, John Gregory Dunne and Joan Didion. It's based loosely on the real-life story of newscaster Jessica Savitch. Sally Atwater (Michelle Pfieffer) gets a job at a Miami TV station based on a demo tape from her hometown of Reno,

Nevada. The station's news director is Warren Justice (Robert Redford), a former high-profile Washington newsman whose career has suffered from his insistence on integrity. He makes Sally his gofer and criticizes her clothes and appearance while she begs him for a chance to go on-air. She becomes the station's weathercaster and Warren gives her the stage name of Tally. With Warren's constant advice, she breaks into news reporting and her star rises quickly as the two become romantically involved. She takes a better job in Philadelphia, with Warren's blessing, and there she soon eclipses the anchorwoman Marcia McGrath (Stockard Channing). From there, Tally's career continues to flourish, while her relationship with Warren takes some strange twists and turns.

Crash (1996) by David Cronenberg

Avge Tomato vs Watcher's Rating: 59%-61%
Fresh-Rotten Reviews: 30-12
After surviving a brutal car wreck, commercial director James Ballard finds himself slowly drawn to a mysterious subculture of people who have transformed automobile accidents into erotic events. Like the J.G. Ballard novel that inspired it, David Cronenberg's study of the sexual dimension of man's relationship to technology was a magnet for controversy, drawing a NC-17 rating and criticism from several sources, including studio owner Ted Turner, who attempted to prevent the film's American release. But though some have leveled charges of pornography, James' descent into this fetishistic underworld is approached with cold, scientific detachment. Characters like Vaughn, the charismatic

group leader who stages recreations of celebrity car crashes, seem more like driven researchers than sexual renegades, which is undoubtedly part of the film's point. This impression is reinforced by the pristine cinematography by Peter Suschitzsky, which proves particularly haunting during a crucial accident scene, and Howard Shore's superb score. Far from exploitative, Crash in fact proves less transgressive than the original novel, but is still undoubtedly not for all tastes. ~ Judd Blaise, Rovi

Ten (2003) by Abbas Kiarostami

Avge Tomato vs Watcher's Rating: 87%-80%
Fresh-Rotten Reviews: 45-7
A drama that consists of a series of ten conversations that take place between the driver of a car, a middle-class Tehran woman in her 30's, and various passengers, including her young son.

Elephant (2003) by Gus Van Sant

Avge Tomato vs Watcher's Rating: 73%-79%
Fresh-Rotten Reviews: 116-43
A tale about high school violence that unfolds on an ordinary school day, inside an American high school, filled with schoolwork, football, gossip and socializing. For each of the students we meet, high school is a different experience: stimulating, friendly, traumatic, lonely, hard.

Mulholland Drive (2001) by David Lynch

Avge Tomato vs Watcher's Rating: 85%
Fresh-Rotten Reviews: 143-30

Along Mulholland Drive nothing is what it seems. In the unreal universe of Los Angeles, the city bares its schizophrenic nature, an uneasy blend of innocence and corruption, love and loneliness, beauty and depravity. A woman (Laura Harring) is left with amnesia following a car accident. An aspiring young actress (Naomi Watts) finds her staying in her aunt's home. The puzzle begins to unfold, propelling us through a mysterious labyrinth of sensual experiences until we arrive at the intersection of dreams and nightmares.

Appreciation

Tropical Malady (2005)
by Apichatpong Weerasethakul

Avge Tomato vs Watcher's Rating: 77%-77%
Fresh-Rotten Reviews: 34-10
One of Thailand's leading experimental filmmakers, Apichatpong Weerasethakul directed this ambitious examination of fear and desire. Keng (Banlop Lomnoi) is a soldier who has been assigned duty as a forest ranger in the woodlands of the country. While on duty, he meets a young man named Tong (Sakda Kaewbuadee); Keng becomes deeply infatuated with Tong, but while Tong is friendly with Keng, he is obviously unwilling to respond to his romantic overtures. As Keng deals with his disappointment, he learns that a number of animals and villagers have fallen victim to a vicious predator who may be a tiger or a shape-shifting shaman. Keng gathers his courage and begins tracking the beast, which alternately resembles a jungle cat and his friend Tong. Sud Pralad (aka Tropical Malady) was screened in competition at the 2004 Cannes Film Festival.

A History of Violence (2005)
by David Cronenberg

Avge Tomato vs Watcher's Rating: 87%-76%
Fresh-Rotten Reviews: 184-27

Tom Stall is living a happy and quiet life with his lawyer wife and their two children in the small town of Millbrook, Indiana, but one night their idyllic existence is shattered when Tom foils a vicious attempted robbery in his diner. Sensing danger, he takes action and saves his customers and friends in the self-defense killings of two-sought-after criminals. Heralded as a hero, Tom's life is changed overnight, attracting a national media circus, which forces him into the spotlight. Uncomfortable with his newfound celebrity, Tom tries to return to the normalcy of his ordinary life only to be confronted by a mysterious and threatening man who arrives in town believing Tom is the man who's wronged him in the past. As Tom and his family fight back against this case of mistaken identity, they are forced to confront their relationships.

War of the Worlds (2005) by Steven Spielberg

Avge Tomato vs Watcher's Rating: 75%-42%
Fresh-Rotten Reviews: 191-65
This is a contemporary retelling of H.G. Wells' seminal sci-fi classic. The adventure/thriller reveals humankind's extraordinary battle against an extra-terrestrial invasion fleet, as seen through the eyes of one American family. Located somewhere in the New England United States, the family is forced to take refuge from the aliens' highly advanced weapons and impenetrable shields.

The New World (2005) by Terrence Malick

Avge Tomato vs Watcher's Rating: 62%-75%
Fresh-Rotten Reviews: 113-69
This epic adventure is set amid the encounter of European and Native American cultures during the founding of the Jamestown Settlement in 1607. Inspired by the legend of John Smith and Pocahontas, this story is a sweeping exploration of love, loss and discovery — both a celebration and an elegy of the America that was... and the America that was yet to come.

The Secret of the Grain (2007) by Kechiche

Avge Tomato vs Watcher's Rating: 92%-76%
Fresh-Rotten Reviews: 49-4

Though it is seldom discussed (or acknowledged) in the West, modern-day France incorporates a substantial number of immigrant communities, with many indigenes from North Africa populating the bucolic regions of southern Gaul. Abdel Kechiche's La Graine et le Mulet hones in on one such community, located on the ocean, which exudes a laid-back, unforced rhythm and a slower pace of life for all of its residents. For many years, one such occupant, sexagenarian Slimane Beiji (Habib Boufares), has nurtured a single lifelong dream: to open up his own couscous and fish restaurant in the community. This dream appears ever more impossible when Slimane is promptly laid off, but he soon lands on the idea of occupying a wrecked boat and converting it into the restaurant. Meanwhile, the gentleman has recently divorced his wife, Souad (Bouraouia Marzouk), and has moved into a hotel owned by his lover, Latifa (Hatika Karaoui), but Slimane's extended family continues to meet at Souad's home on a weekly basis for her beloved fish couscous, where they expostulate their views on life and reflect on the state of their relationships with one another. In a tangentially related subplot, Slimane's oldest son, Hamid (Abdelhamid Aktouche), enjoys an extramarital affair, ignoring his nuptials with his Russian wife and the presence of his infant boy, and thus endangering the sanctity and happiness of his family. ~ Nathan Southern, Rovi

The Host (2007) by Bong Joon-ho

Avge Tomato vs Watcher's Rating: 93%-72%
Fresh-Rotten Reviews: 140-11
When a young girl is snatched away from her father by a horrifying giant monster that emerges from the River Han to wreak havoc on Seoul, her entire family sets out to locate the beast and bring their little girl back home to safety in South Korean director Bong Joon-ho's big-budget creature feature. Hee-bong is a man of modest

means who runs a snack bar on the banks of the River Han. Along with his slow-witted eldest son, Gang-du; Gang-du's young daughter, Hyun-seo; archery champion daughter Nam-joo; and unemployed, shirker son, Nam-il, Hee-Bong has managed to maintain a close relationship with his family despite the hardships that come with being a single father. When a rampaging fiend erupts from the Han and throws the city of Seoul into a state of emergency, Gang-du is heartbroken to see his precious little girl scooped up by the scaly creature and spirited away to an unknown destination. This is one family that always sticks together, though, and as the rest of the city denizens scramble to take cover, Hee-bong, Gang-du, Nam-joo, and Nam-il set out to prove that they're not letting their little girl go without a fight.

Uncle Boonmee... (2011) by Apichatpong Weerasethakul

Avge Tomato vs Watcher's Rating: 89%-60%
Fresh-Rotten Reviews: 86-11
Suffering from acute kidney failure, Uncle Boonmee has chosen to spend his final days surrounded by his loved ones in the countryside. Surprisingly, the ghost of his deceased wife appears to care for him, and his long lost son returns home in a non-human form. Contemplating the reasons for his illness, Boonmee treks through the jungle with his family to a mysterious hilltop cave - the birthplace of his first life... -- (C) Strand.

We Have a Pope (2012) by Nanni Moretti

Avge Tomato vs Watcher's Rating: 65%-55%
Fresh-Rotten Reviews: 52-28
Nanni Moretti joins forces with the great French actor Michel Piccoli to tell the story of Melville, a cardinal who suddenly finds himself elected as the next Pope. Never the front runner and completely caught off guard, he panics as he's presented to the faithful in St. Peter's Square. To prevent a worldwide crisis, the Vatican's spokesman calls in an unlikely psychiatrist who is neither religious or all that committed, played by Moretti, to find out what is wrong with the new Pope.-- (C) IFC

Spring Breakers (2013) by Harmony Korine

Avge Tomato vs Watcher's Rating: 67%-38%
Fresh-Rotten Reviews: 124-62
Brit (Ashley Benson), Candy (Vanessa Hudgens), Cotty (Rachel Korine) and Faith (Selena Gomez) have been best friends since grade school. They live together in a boring college dorm and are hungry for adventure. All they have to do is save enough money for spring break to get their shot at having some real fun. A serendipitous encounter with rapper "Alien" (James Franco) promises to provide the girls with all the thrill and excitement they could hope for. With the encouragement of their new friend, it soon becomes unclear how far the girls are willing to go to experience a spring break they will never forget.

Cosmopolis (2012) by David Cronenberg

Avge Tomato vs Watcher's Rating: 66%-31%
Fresh-Rotten Reviews: 114-60

New York City, not-too-distant-future: Eric Packer, a 28 year-old finance golden boy dreaming of living in a civilization ahead of this one, watches a dark shadow cast over the firmament of the Wall Street galaxy, of which he is the uncontested king. As he is chauffeured across midtown Manhattan to get a haircut at his father's old barber, his anxious eyes are glued to the yuan's exchange rate: it is mounting against all expectations, destroying Eric's bet against it. Eric Packer is losing his empire with every tick of the clock. Meanwhile, an eruption of wild activity unfolds in the city's streets. Petrified as the threats of the real world infringe upon his cloud of virtual convictions, his paranoia intensifies during the course of his 24-hour cross-town odyssey. Packer starts to piece together clues that lead him to a most terrifying secret: his imminent assassination.

Under the Skin (2014) by Jonathan Glazer

Avge Tomato vs Watcher's Rating: 84%-55%
Fresh-Rotten Reviews: 193-36
From visionary director Jonathan Glazer (Sexy Beast, Birth) comes a stunning career transformation, a masterpiece of existential science fiction that journeys to the heart of what it means to be human, extraterrestrial--or something in between. A voluptuous woman of unknown origin (Scarlett Johansson) combs the highways in search of isolated or forsaken men, luring a succession of lost souls into an otherworldly lair. They are seduced, stripped of their humanity, and never heard from again. Based on the novel by Michel Faber (The Crimson Petal and the White), Under The Skin examines human experience from the perspective of an unforgettable heroine who grows too comfortable in her borrowed skin, until she is abducted into humanity with devastating results.

Toni Erdmann (2016) by Maren Ade

Avge Tomato vs Watcher's Rating: 93%-73%
Fresh-Rotten Reviews: 204-15
Practical joker Winfried loves to annoy his daughter with corny pranks. What's worse are his little jabs at her routine lifestyle of long meetings, hotel bars and performance reports. Father and daughter reach an impasse, and Winfried agrees to return home to Germany. Enter flashy "Toni Erdmann": Winfried's smooth-talking alter ego. Disguised in a tacky suit, weird wig and even weirder fake teeth, Toni barges into Ines' professional life, claiming to be her CEO's life coach. As Toni, Winfried is bolder and doesn't hold back, but Ines meets the challenge. The harder they push, the closer they become. In all the madness, Ines begins to understand that her eccentric father might deserve some place in her life after all.

Phantom Thread (2018) by Paul Thomas Anderson

Avge Tomato vs Watcher's Rating: 91%-70%
Fresh-Rotten Reviews: 283-27
Set in the glamour of 1950's post-war London, renowned dressmaker Reynolds Woodcock and his sister Cyril are at the center of British fashion, dressing royalty, movie stars, heiresses, socialites, debutants and dames with the distinct style of The House of Woodcock. Women come and go through Woodcock's life, providing the confirmed bachelor with inspiration and companionship, until he comes across a young, strong-willed woman, Alma, who soon becomes a fixture in his life as his muse and lover. Once controlled and planned, he finds his carefully tailored life disrupted by love. With his latest film, Paul Thomas Anderson paints an illuminating portrait both of an artist on a creative journey, and the women who keep his world running. Phantom Thread is Paul Thomas Anderson's eighth movie, and his second collaboration with Daniel Day-Lewis.

Epilogue

Why Women do not Unite

What surprises me personally, however, is women's apparent[34] inability to act with female solidarity. I apologize for offending some of the possibly better informed female readership. I suggest the most offended women, particularly those *who never moved a finger for improving the social status of less educated women,* to watch some X or R-rated movies by Angelina Jolie. If you do so, please tell me: is Jolie an independent adult, free in her choices, or is she heavily blackmailed, and in urgent need of protection against herself?

Evidently, I do not mean that women, offended or not, should take political initiatives *exclusively* for helping psycho's like Jolie. However, she is but the extreme of a probability tail. If women concentrate their efforts in improving the *median* of the female social status distribution, then the tail reduces mathematically.

The simple answer to the question why women are under-represented in politically highly influential positions

---

34 I add the adverb "apparently", as I may have missed important female efforts

is due to their brain wiring, methinks.[35] Cambridge (UK) professor Simon Baron-Cohen defines three types of brains:

- the S or Systemizing brain;
- the E or Empathic brain;
- the B or Balanced brain

These brain wirings are found in both men and women. However, men are mostly S-wired, while women mostly E-wired. For this reason, S-wired brains are also called male brains, and E-wired brains also female brains.

In my book "feminine feminist" I quote professor Simon Baron-Cohen at length, in order to explain why 30 years of Feminism have brought essentially nothing for women, apart from some absurd laws setting minima to percentages of female participation in highly-ranked jobs. Even a cheese head like me can understand that such laws merely *undermine the dignity of women.*

In "feminine feminist" you also find a proposal for a strategy of a political party defending the rights of women. It is not a particularly smart strategy, but at least it takes into account the average gender-dependent brain-wirings.

---

[35] Nothing to be ashamed of. Men are primarily war machines, women educators.

www.ingramcontent.com/pod-product-compliance
Lightning Source LLC
Chambersburg PA
CBHW061223070526
44584CB00029B/3966